THE GREAT BOOK OF ANIMAL KNOWLEDGE

SEA OTTERS

Seafarers of the Weasel Family

Introduction

Sea otters are the heaviest species of otter in the world. However, despite being heavy, they are incredibly floatable. In fact, they can float all their lives without ever having to go to land! Sea otters are important animals that keep the ecosystem healthy. Sadly, they are now an endangered species. Let's learn more about these interesting and important animals.

What Sea Otters Look Like

Photo by Chris Hunkeler (flickr.com/chrishunkeler), as licensed under CC BY-SA 2.0 Generic

Sea otters are very cute looking animals. They are very furry, and they are colored brown. They have four webbed feet and a tail that is quite flat used to help them swim. They also have retractable claws on each of their feet.

Size and Weight

Sea otters are the smallest marine mammals in the world. They grow around 4 ft (1.25 m) long, which is very small compared to other marine mammals such as whales, dolphins, and walruses. They are, however, the heaviest species of otter. They weigh around 65 pounds (30 kg).

Where Sea Otters Live

Photo by Pacific Southwest Region USFWS (flickr.com/usfws_pacificsw), as licensed under CC BY 2.0 Generic

Sea otters can only be found in the Pacific Ocean. They live on the western coast of North America, from California to Alaska. They can also be found on the eastern coasts of Russia and Japan.

Behavior

Sea otters can walk on land, and sometimes they drag themselves to shore to rest. But they almost exclusively spend their time in the water. They can live without ever having to go to the land.

Swimming

Sea otters are master swimmers. Their bodies are very floatable. Sea otters usually float on their backs and use their webbed feet to move around. It's quite slow when sea otters float on their back; they only travel around 3-5 miles per hour (7-8 km/h). When they need to hurry up, sea otters use their whole body to swim in a wavelike way.

Fur

Sea otters have extremely thick fur. Unlike other marine mammals, they don't have a layer of fat called blubber in their bodies. They rely only on their fur to keep warm. Sea otters have two layers of fur on their bodies. The first layer is a very dense layer of short hairs. So dense, scientists say there can be about 1 million hairs per square inch! The second layer is made of longer hairs. These two layers of fur make the sea otter completely waterproof. No water can touch a sea otters skin!

Grooming

Photo by Pacific Southwest Region USFWS (flickr.com/usfws_pacificsw), as licensed under CC BY 2.0 Generic

For sea otters, grooming is very important. If water touches the skin of a sea otter, it will be very bad; the sea otter can even die if this happens. They have to keep their fur clean and make sure that water can never reach their skin. Sea otters spend lots of time rubbing their fur and splashing in the water.

What Sea Otters Eat

Sea otters are omnivores; which means that they eat both meat and plants. They sometimes eat seaweeds and water plants, but they are mostly meat eaters. Their prey includes sea urchins, crabs, clams, fish, sea snails, and squid.

Diving

Photo by Bart Vetters (flickr.com/robartes), as licensed under CC BY 2.0 Generic

In order to get most of their food, sea otters have to dive down to the sea floor. Sea otters can close their noses and ears when underwater. They usually dive in waters that are around 60 ft (18 m) deep, but they can dive as deep as 300 ft (90 m)! Sea otters can hold their breath for up to five minutes.

Senses

While underwater, sea otters use their whiskers to sense vibrations and find their food. They also rely on their sensitive paws to locate their prey underwater. Aside from those, sea otters also have a good sense of smell and eyesight.

Tools

Sea otters are one of the few animals that use tools to help them. When they catch a clam, they also bring a rock to the surface. They then use the rock to smash the hard shell of the clam open, and then they eat the soft meat inside. Sea otters also tie themselves in kelp, a seaweed that's very long, to anchor themselves in an area.

Drinking

Have you ever wondered how an animal living in the salty ocean drinks water? We can't drink salt water because we will actually become thirstier and dehydrated if we do. Unlike humans, sea otters and other sea mammals have large kidneys that allow them to remove the salt from the water without getting dehydrated. So they can drink from the ocean freely. However, sea otters actually get most of their water needs from the food they eat.

Groups

Sea otters can often be found in a group. These groups are usually male-only or female-only groups, only territorial males can be found with female groups. These groups are called rafts, and the members are often seen resting together.

Breeding

Photo by Pacific Southwest Region USFWS (flickr.com/usfws_pacificsw), as licensed under CC BY 2.0 Generic

Male sea otters are territorial and mate with females within his territory. Female sea otters are often seen with bloody noses during the breeding season because males bite them. Females are pregnant for 6 months before giving birth to usually only one pup. She can only take care of one pup at a time, and will abandon the others if she has more than one.

Baby Sea Otters

Photo by Jodie Wilson (flickr.com/jumpyjodes), as licensed under CC BY 2.0 Generic

Sea otters are the only otters that give birth in the water. Newborn sea otters are already covered in thick fur, and they are so floatable they can't sink! The mother brings her pup around on her chest for about two months. After these two months, the pup will start catching its own food. Sea otters leave their mothers after 6-12 months.

Predators

Photo by Brian Gratwicke (flickr.com/briangratwicke), as licensed under CC BY 2.0 Generic

Sea otters are not the favorite meal of predators because they have scent glands that make them taste bad. However, they still do get killed by other animals. The great white sharks is their main predator. Other predators include killer whales, sea lions, eagles, and bears if they go to the land.

Endangered

Sea otters used to be heavily hunted for their thick fur. So heavily were they hunted that they almost became extinct! Today, there are laws that protect the sea otters and now their population has increased to more than 100,000 sea otters. However, they are still an endangered species.

Subspecies

Photo by frank wouters (flickr.com/frank-wouters), as licensed under CC BY 2.0 Generic

There are three subspecies of sea otters. They all look and act similar, but there are a few differences between them. The three subspecies are the common sea otter found in Russia and Japan, southern sea otter found in California, and the northern sea otter found in Alaska.

Relatives

Sea otters have many other otter relatives such as the giant otter and the river otters. All these otters are part of the weasel family. Other members of the weasel family include weasels, ferrets, minks, and badgers.

Importance

Photo by Joe Ross (flickr.com/joeross), as licensed under CC BY-SA 2.0 Generic

Sea otters are important for the health of the ecosystem. They eat sea urchins and other animals that like to eat kelp. Without sea otters the underwater forests of kelp may disappear, and the many animals that depend on kelp forests as their home will also disappear.

Get the next book in this series!

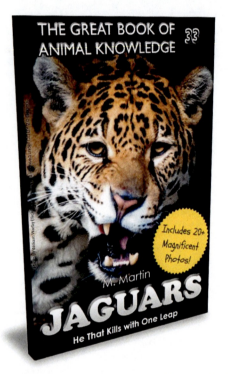

JAGUARS: He That Kills with One Leap

Log on to Facebook.com/GazelleCB for more info

Tip: Use the key-phrase "The Great Book of Animal Knowledge" when searching for books in this series.

For more information about our books, discounts and updates, please Like us on FaceBook!

Facebook.com/GazelleCB

34130191R00015

Made in the USA
San Bernardino, CA
30 April 2019